Forwa

C000172841

Chippy Swingin

A Chippy's experience of sailing on 28 different
ships over a 13 year period in the 50's and 60's of
witnessing some of the Cold War with Russia, the
middle of The Cultural Revolution in China and the
Evils of Apartheid in South Africa.
As well as seeing lots of the British Empire gain
Independence

FOR PHIL EX M/N
BEST WISHES

This is the first publication 2011

ISBN 0 95698490 6

Publisher: Alan Mulvain
17 Vine Street, South Shields
Tyne and Wear NE33 4RF

Printed: by Agrafica NE Ltd
Garden Lane, South Shields
NE33 1PS

email: info@agrafica.co.uk   www.agrafica.co.uk

07917 121 646

ACKNOWLEDGEMENTS

My grateful thanks and appreciation goes to the following people for all the help, advice and patience at various stages on many occasions that helped my book through its journey

I would like to thank my son Brian who initially came up with the idea and arranged various stages and pulled everyone together in order to make this happen

A big thanks goes out to my wife Joyce for all her help and patience Joyce not only re wrote the whole book into a readable text she has also had to listen to all my stories and tales over and over again

A huge thanks to my family especially George and Sharon who helped fund the initial copy and provided me with my best Christmas present ever (The first edition)
Also my grandson Steven for his help on designing the front cover.

Thank you to Joanne Hutchinson of Precious Time, in converting the handwritten copy into computer usable text

Very special thanks to Keith Newman at Highlights Public Relations Ltd for the assistance and support. Press, media photographs, pre & post press release.

Thanks also go to Carl Mowatt M.D. Agrafica NE Ltd for preparing the book ready for publication, innovating new work, amendments and printing

Finally I would like to dedicate this book to all my family and hope they all enjoy it and pass my tales and stories on to future generations.

Chippy Swinging the Lamp
By
Alan Mulvain

The constant battering of the ship against the pounding seas didn't seem to bother the off watch crew as they sat around the old oak table smoking rolled up cigarettes and drinking sweet hot tea. The aroma of stale pipe smoke drifted heavily around the mess room, evidence that old Jack had just left to start his dog watch.

The five remaining shipmates began their nightly ritual of tall tales and yarns, each trying to out tell the tales of the others. Only the swinging of the oil lamp occasionally illuminated the knowing smiles of the shipmates as they swapped tales of monstrous seas, exciting new lands and wild runs ashore in the far flung corners of the world.

Chippy "Swinging the lamp" is Alan Mulvain's personal tales of life at sea from his life as an apprentice on the Tyne to his last ship in the late 1960's.

His tales will lead you into a world of danger, friendship and adventure as well as giving you an insight into life at sea.

How far you want to believe the lamp swings is up

to the discretion and imagination of the reader, so
put on your Wellington boots, grab the binoculars
and set a course for adventure, living history and
traditional Geordie humour.

Introduction

I suppose that right from the start I was destined to go to sea. When your father and four brothers all took the seafaring route, it was inevitable that I would follow in their very wet footsteps. My father Tommy, mother Laura and my brothers Billy, Tommy, Stan and John all lived in a three bed roomed upstairs flat at 19 Temple Street, South Shields, and as well as all the boys I also had a younger sister Joan which made life a bit crowded at times.

Growing up in the 1940's, everyone had an outside toilet, and no bathroom or kitchen to speak of, so it was fairly hectic at times. Looking back it must have been quite an ordeal for my mother, but she always managed, brought us up to know right from wrong and generally coped very well to keep the family together.

One of the advantages of having sea going brothers was that when they joined their ship, there was more room in the flat for me and my sister.

Chapter 1

The sea going life I was to have in front of me would lead to months away from home and I guess to a lot of people that would be hard to take. I however, had a good grounding as I was evacuated during the war with my brother John when I was seven and he was just five years old.

We went to a small village called Haverigg near Millom in Cumbria. I remember that there was a secret Canadian airbase there. We were looked after by a lovely lady called Gladys Burgoyne who worked in the accounts department of the local Co-operative shop. Her job was to take the cash out of the pulley system that whizzed the money from the shop floor to the office. We spent five happy years there; however the downside was never coming home at all and only seeing our parents twice during that time.

Me as a Choir Boy

Gladys with myself and my younger brother John

I made the most of growing up in Haverigg by joining the church choir. I was often taken out of school to sing at the funerals of Canadian airmen that had been killed which brought the far off war very close to me. We were well looked after during our time in Cumbria and I will always remember the kindness Gladys showed to my brother and I.

One night is particularly clear in my memory and I can still see the tears in Gladys's eyes when she was told that her friend and sweetheart was missing in action. He was a dashing Canadian serviceman called Guy from the air force base and I have fond memories of him too.

Guy, Gladys in Girl Guide uniform with the local Scout Master. I also managed to get into the photo too!

I returned to South Shields when I was twelve and kept in touch with Gladys until her death in the 1990's. I went to school at Dean Road School until I was fourteen when I left to become a plasterer. I hated that job and soon left to begin my trade in the boat builder's yard.

Chapter 2

As I previously mentioned, my first taste of working with ships and boats came at the age of fourteen when I became a trainee carpenter in the local ship repair yard on the River Tyne. I served a five year apprenticeship as a shipwright which laid the foundation for my career at sea.

At eighteen, I received my National Service call up papers for the army. As an apprentice serving my time to be a tradesman, I had two options. My choice was that I could opt to serve a two year period in the forces after which my firm was obliged to take me back to finish my apprenticeship, or, service was deferred until I reached the grand old age of twenty one. As it was my ambition to join the Merchant Navy, I opted for the second one. To some people, it would appear that I was trying to avoid conscription, however, under this situation; I had to compulsory stay at sea until I was twenty six. I however stayed at sea until I was thirty six years old.

I carried on repairing ships until three months before I turned twenty one. Time was pressing on as I knew that in three short months I would be in the army unless I acted fast. During my lunch break I would cycle down to the Mill Dam in South

Shields where the seamen were told which ship to embark on. Then I would ask and 'pester' the man who gave out the jobs (if there were any) to see if there were any vacancies for a ships carpenter or, as I was affectionately know "a Chippy".

I suppose I became a constant source of irritation and a pest but eventually he said that there was a job on a British tanker in the Thames, and if I could get my cards back from my firm and be back before four o'clock then the job was mine.

Full of excitement and dreams of new adventures, I raced back to my workplace to ask my foreman if I could have my cards. Unexpectedly to me, he refused point blank. He said that I was serving my time and that there was no way I would be released until I was twenty one. Panic set in, my dreams were fast disappearing but somehow I managed to pluck up enough courage to go to the office and asked to see the manager.

After explaining my situation with the army and also that I had been lucky enough to get a jump (ship), he eventually agreed to release me. I then raced back to the shipping federation, received a railway warrant and a clearance from the Union and I was on my way.

After picking up my toolbox at work, I went home to tell my mother to pack my suitcase as I was leaving that night. After years of experience with my father and brothers, my mother always knew exactly what to pack into the small leather case. Although I never knew what was in my suitcase until I got onboard the ship, I discovered that my mother never left anything out.

Knowing that my sea going adventure was about to start, I went down to the local club to meet my friends and have a few drinks before I left. The bar closed at ten o'clock in those days so after closing time, one of my friends came down to the railway station to carry my tool box for me. He was a 6 foot tall docker, which was handy, as my tool box was very heavy and I would have really struggled if I'd been alone.

Having a beer with my brothers

There is nothing quite like travelling on a steam train and in those days, the LNER's main East Coast Main Line operated some of the most magnificent railway locomotives. The smell of oil and steam billowing from the engine's chimney was a taste of the constant smells to come on board my first ship. The overnight train to "the smoke" or London as its better known was my first journey to an adventure spanning almost thirteen years and covering many thousands of miles.

I was a little apprehensive arriving in London at such a young age and I expected a few surprises, but I was not prepared for the shock I was to receive so soon in my seafaring career.

On arriving in Kings Cross, I had to find my way to the shipping office in Tilbury. I jumped into a taxi cab and as the driver drove off, he asked "where to guv?" in his cockney twang, so I told him Tilbury. I was then told that Tilbury was a long way away and was asked if I had enough money for the fare? I couldn't believe how rude the driver was as he pulled over to the side of the road and practically threw me out of the cab. If this was an example of London hospitality, this wet behind the ears Geordie would rather head back up north where everyone looked after each other.

Thankfully a passing policeman took me to a bus stop on the right side of the road and pointed me in the general direction for Tilbury. After being helped on and off, numerous red Double Decker buses, I finally managed to get to Tilbury and with the huge tool box on my shoulder and my suitcase in my hand; I walked the remainder of the way. After finding the Shipping Office, the Officer sent me to have my photograph taken and arranged for a doctor to ensure that I was medically fit. I was then given my Seaman's Identity Card and Discharge Book.

This was a very proud moment for me; at last I was part of the British Merchant Navy. I decided to celebrate by watching the fireworks from a nearby Guy Fawkes Bonfire display imagining that the firecrackers were exclusively for my benefit, telling the world that at last Alan Mulvain had carried on the family tradition of seafaring. Yes, November 5th 1953 was a very special day as I climbed the rickety gangplank onto my first ship The British Harmony.

Chapter 3

I was so proud of my new home and workplace. The British Harmony was an 8,500 ton oil tanker owned by the British Tanker Company. Built in 1941, she had seen active service during the war and had carried oil many thousands of miles across the world's oceans. I had an immediate connection with her as she was built just six miles away from my home in South Shields at the famous Swan Hunters shipyard on the Tyne at Wallsend. Living proof that "wherever ya gan yell always find a Geordie."

On stepping on board, I was told that my first duty was to 'sound the ship.' This was to see how much freshwater had been used that day and to make certain that there was no water leaking on board. This was to be my first duty every single day on every ship I was on. A kind hearted apprentice showed me how to check the pipes to make sure everything was in order.

With a lot of excitement and anticipation, we sailed next day from the Isle of Grain (which was an oil refinery on the Medway) for Kuwait. My job was to standby on the fore deck to run the windlass, which was used to pick up the anchor when in gear, or run the drum ends when out of gear. Sailing for the Thames after the crew had stowed the ropes away, I noticed that I was now alone on the ship's forecastle. The mate had already told me that it was my job to standby until we dropped off the pilot, and to be prepared in case we had to let go of the anchor.

Imagine how I felt, as a young lad very much alone tasked with dropping the anchor if things went wrong. As I'd never done that job before it did make me very nervous. Thankfully, we entered the open sea without incident and before being stood down by the mate, I was given one more essential job to do. To stop water getting into the anchor chain locker, I had to cement around the anchor cables creating a seal impenetrable by the rough waves to come. After doing all that I was ready to turn in and I had completed my first day at sea without any mishap.

I soon got into the ships routine, mainly by keeping everything greased up and working and doing any repairs that were needed. It was a busy regime but after a hard watch, it was always good to relax with the rest of the crew.
Sometimes after work the crew, who were not on watch, would sit around the mess table telling tale tales and yarns (swinging the lamp). As it was less than a decade after the end of the war, there

were many fascinating tales of bravery, fear and personal tragedy. Three of my shipmates had been torpedoed, one of them twice. I never heard any of them complain about this, even though many of their friends and shipmates had been lost. What I did find very hard to understand was how the government of the time could stop a sailors pay as soon as their ship sank, no one was paid for being in a lifeboat. Now this was bad enough if you were single, but if you were married, your wife's money was also stopped. This to me seemed an injustice, people risking their lives for King and Country and receiving no pay impacting directly on your wife and children as if things weren't bad enough.

Whilst swapping yarns, I was asked what I did during the war. I had to tell them I had been evacuated for five years to Cumbria, so they said 'oh you poor little evacuee', which made me feel very young and a little sheepish.

The passage towards Kuwait was very exciting being my first trip. Passing through the notoriously rough seas of the Bay of Biscay I couldn't help thinking about the famous sailors like Drake and Nelson that had sailed these very seas themselves hundreds of years ago? On we went past the Royal Naval base at Gibraltar with the giant rock towering above the port and the cheeky monkeys posing for tourists photographs we entered the warm and inviting Mediterranean Sea.

Eventually, we reached Port Said, which was the entrance to the Suez Canal. Having arrived, I at last got the chance to drop the anchor as we waited for permission to enter the canal as part of a never ending convoy of tankers, tramp steamers and passenger ships.

To the less nautically minded, dropping the anchor may appear to involve just that. A big metal hook is dropped over the side to stop the ship from moving. It is a bit more technical than that however as tides, weather and the type of material found on the sea bed all have to be taken into consideration. After using the navigator's chart to find a good location, the crew needs to see what the situation is like; are there other vessels in the immediate area? Where will the wind pull the ship?

Once the location is decided upon, the anchorage should be approached from down wind or down current, whichever is stronger. As the chosen spot is approached, the vessel should be stopped. The anchor should be lowered quickly but under control until it is on the bottom. This is where I contributed to the operation by applying the geared braking system when ordered to do so by the Mate. The vessel should continue to drift back, and the cable should be veered out under control so it will be relatively straight.

Once the desired length of chain is laid out (about three times more than the depth of water), the vessel should be gently forced astern until it stops dead in the water. Regular navigation fixes on the chart will reassure the mate that the anchor has a steady hold on the ship. The anchor being released was a milestone in my career and another obstacle to cross off the list of experiences to experience. It was not long before we moved on into the harbour to pick up the light to guide us through the canal. This consisted of a wooden box that was hung over the bow of the ship in which two men would sit in to control the light. Later on of course, each ship would have integral spotlights fitted, but these were early days and we had to improvise with the limited technology we had. We also picked up two boats with two men called Foyboatmen in each to tie us up later on in the canal.

The Suez Canal is a great place to experience the local bartering and trade systems. We had the equivalent of a mobile shop come alongside us and we called these small vessels piled high with goods "bum boats." This boat was run by a man called George Robey, I never knew if that was his real name or not, but anyway that was what we called him. When the bum boat came alongside, everybody on the ship could buy some gear, like underwear, souvenirs, or the likes, and the Captain would pay Mr Robey and then take everyone's bill off their wages account.

We then joined the convoy and sailed on through the canal. The Suez Canal is an artificial sea-level waterway in Egypt, connecting the Mediterranean Sea and the Red Sea. Opened on November 1869, it allows water transportation between Europe and Asia without ships having to navigate around Africa. The canal is 119 miles long and for most of that distance it is only possible for single file passage to take place although there are one or two passing places.
When another faster ship wanted to overtake us or if a convoy traveling in the opposite direction wanted to pass by us, we were tied up by the boatmen who we had taken on board. From our tie up position, you could not see the canal, but to see this line of huge ships pass as if sailing on the desert was quite an impressive sight.

After the westward convoy had passed, we moved on to the Bitter Lakes which were huge saltwater lakes in the middle of the canal, and dropped anchor to await our turn. Whilst in the lakes, some of us decided to have a swim as it was quite warm. Now I am not a particularly good swimmer, but I decided to swim around the ship. When I got halfway around I realised that this was the point of no return and I was really struggling. Somehow, I managed to keep going, egged on by some of the crew hanging over the ships rail. Now they might have thought it was funny, but believe me, I did not and I will never know how I got back to the accommodation ladder. That was the last attempt at circumnavigating my ship from the water that I ever did!

We weighed anchor and sailed through the canal to Port Suez, where we dropped the boats and lights before sailing down the Red Sea past Aden and on to Kuwait. While there you were not allowed to go ashore, but you were given a glass of iced orange juice and that was your lot. I was very disappointed; after weeks at sea, I had travelled all those miles for a drink of orange.

The turnaround was so fast and caught me by surprise. No sooner had we tied up in Kuwait and we were back on route to England again. The whole process of loading crude oil only took a few hours and then it was back into the sea going routine once more.

Part of the routine was to change bed linen on a Saturday. This was where I came across class distinction. White sheets and pillowcases for Petty

Officers, like me, and blue lined for the rest of the crew. We even had different soap, Lux toilet soap for the PO's and Lifebuoy for the crew. I don't think it was any cheaper, but you always had to have class on ships. On Saturdays you cleaned your cabin, made everything shipshape, ready for inspection on Sunday morning. After the Captain had made the inspection, the Petty Officer's would be given a shot of rum from the Captain, unfortunately, there was nothing given to the rest of the crew.

On arriving back to the Isle of Grain, we discharged the ship before sailing up the North Sea to dry dock at North Shields on the River Tyne. This was my home port, which made it very handy. The ship then paid off and I had completed my very first trip at sea.

Chapter 4

By now it was time to take a bit of leave, so I decided to buy a radio, with short wave to take away with me. I spent a considerable time shopping for the smallest one I could find. I managed to find one of reasonable size, but it was not that small as this was before the transistor was invented, and as it was a value radio, I also had to take a transformer to change the home voltage of 240 watts to the ships 110 watts, so much for a portable radio!

On Sunday nights we would go along to the workingman's club to see a concert party. This usually consisted of a number of variety acts, which were always very entertaining. At ten o'clock, closing time, we all had to stand to attention for the Queen. The committee made sure you obeyed this rule; in fact it was almost a hanging offence not to do so. This could turn out to be a good thing, as at least it proved after drinking all night you were still capable of standing up.

We never had television then, as it was something new and very few people owned one. We did not even have a proper radio, but rented a speaker from Redifusion, which was wired into the house, so we could receive the BBC and Radio Luxembourg.

My father loved music, and Radio Luxembourg played the top 20 records every Sunday night, so we all listened to the hit parade as it was called in those days. My father at the time was sailing on a collier, after spending most of the war years supplying the Royal Navy in Scapa Flow in the Orkney's to the far north of Scotland.

A collier was used to ship coal from the North East to the power stations of London. As this was not such a long journey, he managed to get home every week end. We used to have a dartboard on the sitting room door, so we could play darts or cards with whoever happened to be at home at the time, so that was the way our family life was at that time. Perhaps the present generation could learn from that, as now everyone seems to live in their own little world of TV, surfing the net or playing with the latest electric gadgets.

Chapter 5

After a welcome break, it was time to try and find another ship, so I went back over the river to North Shields, where I had left my last ship, and saw the Superintendent of the British Tanker Company, which was the company's name then. Later it changed its name to BP and became one of the biggest names in the petroleum business.

There was four British tankers in the repair yard at that time, so I was offered a position on one that was about to sail. My next ship was the British Marquis and on the 26 February 1954, I set sail bound for Dacca in the Indian Ocean.

This ship also had a North Eastern connection having been built at the Doxford Yard in Sunderland in 1946. At nearly 500 feet long and 8,500 tons the British Monarch was a good solid ship.

On the long days and nights at sea, I would try and get some reception on my radio. I would do this by climbing the mast and make some weird shape for the aerial, without much success; however on reaching Port Said, I found that I could tune in to the British Service Network. At this time, the British Forces were stationed there to patrol and protect the canal, so we sailed right into the heart of the noise and bustle.

At Port Said, you had to be very careful to keep the Gypsy's and thieves out of your cabin as if anything was not fastened down, they would steal it. We then sailed through the canal and I would watch the Boatmen smoke the Hubbly Bubbly, which was a pipe with a long tube that passed through a jar containing water. This was to cool the smoke. I do not know what it is they smoked, but it didn't smell like tobacco.

We then sailed onto Dacca via the Indian Ocean and into the Bay of Bengal to arrive in Dacca, which was in India, and is now a part of Bangladesh. So at last, I was able to go ashore, but not for very long, as tankers had a quick turn around. Our next destination was Venice and off we set again for the Suez.

Significantly, this was last time that I was to use the canal for a while, as in 1956 Colonel Nassa, who was the Egyptian President at the time, nationalised the canal to fund the building of the Aswan Dam. The UK then invaded to claim it back, but Anthony Eden, who was Prime Minister, was made to stand down by the United Nations, mainly through the influence of the USA. The Egyptians blocked the canal, by sinking ships, and at the time, some ships were stuck in the Bitter Lakes and had to remain there for the duration of the conflict along with their crew's.

On route to Venice, our engine blew up off the Island of Crete. Often, we would stop for a running repair, but this was too big a job, as the crank shaft was twisted, so we had to radio for help and a small coaster tanker belonging to the company came to our rescue and helped us as we were drifting towards the rocks.

The way we got a line on board was to use a forty gallon drum and drift a line over to the ship. This seemed a bit amateurish, but it was effective. Towing a ship at sea can be very dangerous and I was always mindful of standing too close to a tight hawser rope which could snap at any time.
A larger ship from the company came to tow us back to the UK, we had to anchor off and use the cables, as well as towing springs to keep the two ships as far apart as possible, and so we began the long journey home. We received a radio message to say the Queen and Prince Philip were on the Royal Yacht Britannia, on the way to Australia, and would be passing close by and we had to alter course to make sure that there was no danger to them. We must have been someway off, because we never saw them.

Weeks and weeks passed as we were only making two to three knots, and eventually we arrived off the Isle of White to be picked up by two powerful tugs from Hull that took us to the Isle of Grain to discharge, and on to Sunderland on the River Wear for engine repairs.

So we then paid off and I thought that I had had enough of tankers, it was a good way to save money, because you never got a chance to get ashore to spend it and I had not gone to sea to save, but rather to spend, and see some of the World. As all really seen of the world was the sea, I made a decision to try and get a cargo ship to improve my prospects by broadening my horizons and finding out more about the world.

Unlike tankers where you signed on per voyage, on a cargo ship, you signed on for two years, and you had to stay there until your contract was up. The only way you could pay off was if the ship came back to the UK, and it was your final port of discharge, which meant if you went to the Australian coast, for instance, you had to stay for two years before heading home, which a lot of ships did then, so that was quite a long trip in the ships articles. You also signed to ply between 7000 north and 7000 south, areas of extreme cold and ferocious seas.

Chapter 6

I signed up to my first cargo vessel the MV La-
pama. The ship was to pick up a cargo in Northern
Russia, and then sail in to the Arctic Ocean, beyond
the 7000 north latitude. The ship was due a complete crew change and I had to travel to London to
pick them up. My orders were to make my way to
the east end of London, and to stay in the Flying
Angel, which was the Seaman's Mission, quite basic accommodation, but comfortable. While I was
in the Mission, I was to see my first television and
the place was crowded, as we all gathered round
the small black and white set to see the final of the
1954 World Cup. I think it was the first World Cup
to be televised and West Germany won Hungary
3-2.

The shipping agent assembled the crew, from all
walks of life and we set off on a bus for Dover.
The ship had not yet arrived, so we had three or
four hours to wait. Most of the men went to a pub
and by the time the ship dropped anchor in the
harbour and transported the outgoing crew ashore,
there were quite a few of the new crew, a little
worse for wear. It was quite funny to see the agent
trying to round everyone up and join the launch
to take them out into the harbour, but everyone
eventually managed to get on board. I had a lot of

doubts about the new crew – many of which became realised later in the passage. This was the 5th July 1954.

We set sail for Rotterdam in Holland to discharge and take on stores. Rotterdam is a long way up river, but at that time of year, the weather was alright, so my long standby passed without incident. I had doubts about the competency and integrity of some of the crew from when I first met them and it turned out that the seaman who was at the wheel did not know how to steer at all. He was a taxi driver, and had somehow the authorities about his qualifications and experience.

When we took on stores and while loading, the crew managed to steal two crates of whiskey. Naturally, the Captain was not very happy about this and I think he was beginning to worry about what kind of crew he had taken onboard. But there was worse to come. After taking on stores, we moved on down the river into the North Sea sailing past Norway and into the Barents Sea and on to Murmansk. This was at the height of the Cold War and we were boarded and searched by the Russians in Murmansk, a port where there seemed to be hundreds of Soviet navy warships.

We eventually cut through the red tape and got clearance and sailed on into the Barents Sea. By that time we had a Russian Ice Pilot. One day we passed a huge polar bear on the ice flow. It was busy eating a seal, right along the side of the ship, but we did not seem to bother him at all. As we passed, he just hopped off the iceberg into the water with his mouth and ice covered in blood; it was quite a gruesome but totally natural sight. We then cut our way through the ice with the help of the pilot, into the White Sea, and up beside Archangel, to load timber bound for the UK.

The Russian armed guards were everywhere and we were getting into trouble with them all of the time. The ship was being loaded by what the Russians called displaced persons, but I thought that they were probably prisoners of war that they had picked up, as they went through Europe. The displaced persons lived in a compound many thousands of miles from their homelands and I don't suppose they ever got back to their families and friends.

When accounting for the cargo, young girls would fraternise with the crew much to the annoyance of the armed Russian guards.

On the opposite side of the river to our berth there was a Russian military airfield, and one night two of the crew stupidly decided to go for a swim in the river. Lowering a rope ladder over the aft end they descended into the icy river and set off towards the other side. Two armed guards ran aboard and began firing shots over their heads, which could have easily ended in tragedy as the soldiers certainly meant business. When the Captain was alerted to all of the commotion he ordered them to get back on board, and informed them that they would be (logged) fined.

The two men had been heavily drinking; they climbed back onboard and proceeded to kick the Captain's door down. For this stupid action they were given a bad discharge, which prevented them from ever going back to sea again. My suspicions about the motley crew came true once again. My radio also attracted the wrong sorts too as I was the only one on board who owned one. This meant that I was kept awake a lot of nights by shipmates wanting to drink and listen to music in my cabin.

While loading the ship, a preventor parted on one of the Derricks, which caused it to swing into the after end of the bridge, causing a lot of damage and the need for me to do a lot of repairs to do on the homeward voyage. After finishing loading, we then sailed on through the White Sea into the Bright Sea, along the Norwegian Coast. Because we were loaded with timber, and having a deck cargo, it made the ship, what we called – tender, which means it was a bit unstable. Not wishing to lose any of the deck cargo, it meant we had to hug the coast, which gave us a chance to sail through the beautiful Norwegian Fiords, a truly magnificent sight. I was very pleased to get the opportunity to see them. During the passage, a Norwegian trawler came along side and the Chief Steward gave the fishermen some bottles of vodka, for a basket of fish. We enjoyed a nice fresh fish supper that night with a backdrop of mountains and deep blue fjords which made everything perfect. Unfortunately, my lasting impression of Norway was somewhat different.

Chapter 7

I had been working hard to repair the damage done by the Derrick, and as I stood on the handrail to drill a hole to fasten off an awning spar, I went over backwards, did a somersault and landed on the deck below, breaking both my arms and splitting my lip open. The ship diverted into the Port of Kristiansand and put me ashore. I was placed on a stretcher where I was warned by the Captain to make sure the stretcher was sent back to the ship. I was in too much pain to worry about that, so I never found out if it was ever returned by the hospital.

On arrival at the hospital, I was placed in a corridor to wait for a surgeon. I asked a doctor to give me something for the pain, because I had been concussed. He refused to do that. I finally got into the operation theatre where I was anesthetised. The method they used to give anaesthetic involved placing a cotton wool pad over my mouth and pouring ether or chloroform onto it and I was swallowing this stuff! I thought I was going to choke to death, but as I could not do anything, the way my arms were I was completely helpless. They then started to straighten my right wrist, which was at right angles, and I could feel everything they were doing. I tried to tell them that I was not under, but because of the pad over my mouth, I could not get them to understand. I eventually passed out, but I think it was more shock than anaesthetic. When I awoke, I found myself in a hospital bed, trussed up like a chicken. The nurses were all young girls who lived in the hostel in the hospital grounds and having two broken arms, they had to see to my every need, as well as my toilet needs. They had to shave me, clean my teeth and feed me. Now this was at times very embarrassing, sometimes funny, but never dull.

The nurses would spoon feed me pickled raw fish and some kind of sour milk. As the girls could not speak any English, and I could not speak Norwegian I couldn't tell them that I was not enjoying this type of food. To be honest, I had a job to keep it down, but the alternative was to spit it out, which would not have been very nice or polite to my carers. I had no choice, but to suffer and swallow it. When the doctor did his rounds, (he could speak English), I asked him if they had any meat in the hospital, but he explained that they had to live on their natural reserves. In the town, there were a few girls from Liverpool who had married Norwegian seamen. One day two of them came to visit me and brought me some books written in English. After they had left, one of the nurses put one of the books on a frame over the bed and for the next couple of weeks, before I could move my right hand; I would read the same page over and over again until some nurse would pass by and turn a page. How I hated that book. I think was by Dennis Wheatley and I never got to finish it.

The nurses were very good to me and sometimes after duty they would come and sit on my bed. One of them had a guitar and she would play songs for me that helped to pass the time. They also had to give me bed baths, which meant sponging me down all over. After a while, they could tell that I was getting well. They must have told Sister, because they stopped doing it, which was a real shame. I sort of looked forward to the bed baths. After three weeks, I could use my right hand enough to wash myself, shave and go to the toilet, and although I still had both arms in plaster, they decided I was fit enough to travel home by myself. I was booked a passage on a small coaster passenger ship travelling north to Bergen. I had to join this ship in the middle of the night and the young nurses came to the ward and made a fuss of me, dressed me and gave me a right good send off. They had been really good to me.

On the coaster, they had buffet style meals and as no one could speak English, and I couldn't point to what I wanted to put on my plate, I had a problem, but other passengers helped me over this and I managed to eat.

The ship docked in Bergen and as it was to lay up for engine repairs, I asked if I could live on board for a couple of days. They let me have my cabin, so that helped a lot, as I did not have to book into a hotel, which would have been a bit awkward, as I still had a bit of a problem eating ashore.

The next day I went along to the British Consul to see if they could arrange for me to get a passage on the ferry that was going to the River Tyne, after phoning the ferry company, they said the ship was fully booked and there was only a stateroom left. I then explained my predicament that I could not afford to stay in Bergen to wait for the next ship, so they allowed me to have the stateroom. The following day while waiting to join the ferry, a rather brash American explained to everyone loudly that this ship that we were boarding was only a tiny boat compared to what he was used to, as he had travelled on all of the great liners of the World. He saw me and shouted – 'What happened to you Limmey?' I do not know why, but I t said I had been over in Norway boxing and had thought I was winning, but was caught with a soccer punch and was knocked clean out of the ring, and as my face was not completely healed, and thanks to the broken arms, he seemed to swallow this.

I had already told the British Consul that I did not wish to eat in the first class saloon, so they arranged for me to have a book of vouchers to buy my meals with and to hand over any left over at the end of the trip. I then found out I could buy drinks with the vouchers. So needless to say I didn't hand any back. After joining the ship I met up with a young Norwegian couple, a dentist and his wife and we enjoyed the passage together.

The Norwegian couple were immigrating to the USA, and were on their way to Southampton to join a ship called The United States, to take them to America. I remember reading about how the United States took the coveted Blue Riband from Cunard's Queen Elizabeth. This was an award for the fastest ship to cross the Atlantic from Southampton to New York. The dentist shared a cabin with five others not including his wife who never had a room; she just had to sleep on a chair in the lounge. Being the perfect gentleman, I gave her my stateroom, which also had a bathroom and we settled down so spend the rest of the night having a few drinks.

The next day, I decided to send a telegraph home, to let them know when I was due to arrive. To reach the radio office I had to go up to the top deck, which was cordoned off, as it was for first class passengers only. At the top of the ladder, the brash American was lying on a sun chair covered with a

rug, and he shouted loudly enough for other passengers to hear him say," Sorry Limmey but this part of the ship is restricted to first class passengers only"
I asked him if class was given by cabin numbers, he explained that was true, all the low numbers were first class and he was in cabin 25. I then said," I'm in cabin 2, the stateroom, how does that grab you yank?" The deck hand removed the velvet rope to let me pass, and gave me a knowing wink. As I passed I showed him my key number, so that kind of evened up the score with the American. I then went along to the radio officer who sent a telegram by Morse code to my mother. I found out later that it was a waste of time as they did not deliver telegrams on a Sunday, so there was no one there to meet me at North Shields when we docked.

So near to home and yet so far, there I was stuck on a Jetty, with two broken arms in plaster, a small grip to carry, no money and no transport to get home. A bus finally came down to the ship and the driver asked me what had happened, so I explained my situation and although it was out of his way, he took me to the Shields ferry to cross the river to South Shields. My mother was a bit surprised to see me, overjoyed that I was home but upset about my condition.

Chapter 8

After spending about four months being patched
up with physiotherapy and exercise, I was passed
fit by the doctor to return to sea. After celebrat-
ing Christmas at home, I travelled down to the
smoke to Poplar on the Thames to join the Baron
Inverclyde on the 11 January 1955.

We sailed across the Atlantic, which we called the
pond, for the Dominican Republic. In the West
Indies this country is part of the Island of
Hispaniola. The other part of the island belongs to
Haiti. We sailed along the coast and dropped
anchor off a small village to wait to go alongside to
load sugar for the UK. While at anchor the Captain
went ashore and demanded a horse driven carriage
as well as all the drinks he needed and a choice of
girls for free, otherwise no one on that ship would
get any money. As the village needed the business,
needless to say he got what he wanted; a ship's

Captain was very powerful in those days. I was really pleased to get ashore to enjoy the hospitality of my first Caribbean Island.

After loading, we sailed across the Pond again for Purfleet near Tilbury to discharge the sugar for Tate & Lyle. On board a ship you could buy cigarettes very cheaply at the time, you could get 600 for a pound, so I decided to take some home for my brothers. On tying up at Purfleet, I thought I would take my toolbox to the railway station, so I put 400 cigarettes in the till of my tool box and with the help of the Ship's Cadet, set off to walk to the railway station.

On the way, we passed four customs men going down to the ship. After we passed them, one turned round and asked if we were off the ship down the jetty. When we said we were, he asked what was in the box, and I told him just tools. He asked me to open it and I tried to stall him by saying that the key was in my cabin on board. Unfortunately, he made me carry it back to the ship. I then asked if I could leave it on the gangway as it was heavy. He agreed and followed me to my cabin, where I made quite a show of finding the key in the draw. He again asked me if there was anything else in the box, I kept answering just tools. As he bent down to open the box and then the till he saw the cigarettes. He looked up at me and that look was something special. He then asked if I was some kind of a comedian, but he was not laughing. He fined me £10.00. As I was only on thirty pounds a month, this left me without enough money to take a leave, so I went and told the Captain what had happened. He called me a fool, or words to that effect, and signed me on for another trip. So after a few nights in Silvertown, I headed once more across the pond, this time for Cuba.

Chapter 9

At this time, Cuba was under control of a dictator-
ship called Batista. It would be another four years
before Fidel Castro came to power and almost
caused the third World War. I enjoyed Cuba as a
good run ashore, although there was some fighting
in the mountains in the south east, and the Dockers
were saying that come the revolution things would
be very different. I never thought then how true this
was to become.

From Cuba, we sailed south east to Port au Prince
in Haiti, which is on the island of Hispaniola. Everything in this place seemed to belong to one man
and his photograph was everywhere. It was alright
ashore, but certainly different, so we finished loading sugar and sailed across the Pond again for the
UK and this time to pay off in Tilbury.

When I got home on leave I found out that one
of my brothers had jumped ship in Australia, and
was working his way across the country. He managed to work his passage on a ship to get him back
home. My eldest brother at that time was serving
as third engineer on a ship and arrived home while
I was still on leave to be told there was a vacancy
for a Chippy on his ship and would I ship out with
him. I agreed and so I joined the King David on

the 28 April 1955 at Immingham near Hull, which seamen called Ming Ming. We set sail for the USA, eventually dropping anchor in Chesapeake Bay. This was a huge bay with Virginia on one side and Maryland on the other, it was famous for oysters, crabs and clams and lots were caught while we were there.

When we were there, there were dozens of World War Two Liberty Ships lying at anchor, as well as the latest aircraft carriers and submarines. When we dropped anchor in the bay, the emigration officers came out to interrogate us asking silly questions like 'was your father or grandfather ever a member of the communist party?' They also had a short arm inspection, which meant you dropped your trousers to see if you had a sexual disease, this took sometime and the crew were getting a bit fed up. Someone shouted out that you should inspect us when we leave your poxy country. For this he was refused a shore pass, the Officers and Petty Officers did not have to take part in this short arm inspection. They seemed to think we were above that sort of thing.

We then loaded coal for Zeebruge in Belgium to be shipped to the UK. Coal was king at that time. I stayed on the run for six months. Zeebruge is on the mole in Belgium, and while the ship was there, we would go to the town of Blankenburge. This was a seaside holiday town so it was a good run ashore. At some stage, my brother was cautioned for going ashore with me by the captain, as he was an officer and I was a petty officer and he did not think it was right that we should mix. Needless to say, my brother ignored him. After a few trips my brother paid off sick. I gave him some money so that between us we could buy our first television for home. I had to stay on board until the ship came to Barry Docks in Wales, where I paid off. When we paid off, we would get paid in white five pound notes. These notes were quite big with beautiful black scrolling writing and because of the large denomination; sometimes you had a bit of a job to change them. For five pounds in those days, you could buy one hundred pints of beer so you could tell it was quite a lot of money.

While in a bar which was used a lot by seamen and where the staff were accustomed to seeing the five pound note, I pulled out a joke five pound note which was twice the size of a normal one. The barmaid knew I had just paid off, so when I passed off the fun note, she did not bother to unfold it and gave me my change. After a couple of hours, I asked her to check her till, and the five pound note that I had passed over. When she found out what had happened, she gave me a right roasting and was not amused at all. After that I used to call her Vicky after the Old Queen Victoria.

After a spell ashore, I then joined the SS Southwich sailing out of Middlesbrough on the 16 December 1955. The Southwich was an old empire boat built during the war to replace the ships that had been sunk during the war by the U Boats. This ship was a right old rust bucket. The carpenters shop had been washed overboard, so I had to use the Gunners Quarters. The ship was swarming with cockroaches, no matter how hard you tried, you could not get rid of them and they seemed to get everywhere. The engine was not very reliable and the engineers were forever working on it. We managed to chug along as far as the Bay of Biscay where it packed up altogether. The bay is not the best of places to be at any time, but in the middle of December, it can be pretty comfortable, so there we were just wallowing until the engineer managed to fix the engine and get us underway again. We then headed for Monrovia in Liberia to load iron ore. Liberia was established as a home for freed American Slaves by America. The run ashore was much the same as the surrounding countries. After loading we then sailed back to Middlesbrough, where I was not sorry to leave this ship.

Chapter 10

My next ship was to be 'The Sugar Refiner' which I joined on the 1 March 1956, and sailed from Tilbury bound for Jamaica. This ship was built for the D Day Landings and continued to carry sugar for Tate & Lyle. She was a very slow ship, and could not get across the Atlantic without calling at the Azores for water for the boiler. We then sailed on to Jamaica to load sugar. Loading sugar was a very slow process. First of all using the ships riggers, they would pick up the sacks of sugar that had come from the plantations in all kinds of old trucks. After landing them near the hold, the Dockers would then empty them into the hold. As you can imagine the first few sacks that went into the hold just disappeared and looking down, you got the impression that this would take forever, and indeed, took about six weeks to load up. This proved to be an advantage, as you got a chance to see quite a bit of the local area.

I settled down to enjoy my stay in Kingston Town. At that time, it was under British Rule and it would be another six years before it gained independence in 1962. But everyone seemed to be happy enough at the time although now it has a very different if not menacing feel about it. However, the travel agencies then were trying to encourage West Indian people to emigrate to the UK, and the posters in the streets were telling them to how wonderful the UK, was and all they had to do was get there and they would have no need to work anymore, as the British Government would keep them for the rest of their lives, and some of them did just that.

So after loading up, we sailed once again for the UK. After a few days leave, I signed on to the same ship again. It was not a bad job and I was enjoying the run to the West Indies. This time we sailed further south to Trinidad, calling first at the capital Port of Spain and then further down the coast to a sugar plantation. This was another lively run ashore as we were in port with a Royal Fleet Auxiliary ship, which was a Royal Navy Ship crewed by the Merchant Navy.

One night we were all together in a nightclub when one of the crew had seen a girl he knew and claimed he had caught a sexual disease off her. He went to hit her and someone else threw a glass at him, which started a right old barney. Some of the local men waded in with baseball bats. There was quite a lot of damage. I heard the next day that there were a few broken bones and one of the sailors had lost an eye. At the time I was on the balcony and I was seriously thinking of jumping off, but I managed to see a gap in the battle and made my way to the stairs. When I reached ground level, the police were there and I told them they were killing each other in the nightclub. They said they knew and would go in when it was all over. Trinidad proved a bit lively for me so afterwards, when we docked at Tilbury, I left the ship.

Chapter 11

This time when I arrived home, my two younger
brothers were on leave, but when there leave was
up, instead of going to the shipping office, to look
for another ship, they decided to have an extra couple of weeks at home. So they got a job in a ship
repair yard for two weeks. This only lasted one
week before they were called up to the army. This
was the end of their seafaring career for a while.
The authorities did not mess around in those days.

My next ship was to be a new one which was built
in my home town by John Readhead and sons
of South Shields with the added bonus of being
manned with a local crew as well. I signed on to
the SS Baron Ogilvy on the 23 July 1956. This
was my second Baron Ship and they were owned
by Hogarth Brothers. The company ships had a
nickname of the Hungry Hogarths and they richly
deserved their name thanks to the meagre supplies
and limited home comforts on board. Thankfully
we never starved and I began to enjoy the voyage to my next new destination Durban on the east
coast of Africa.

Durban is a port in Natal Province, in the Inde-
pendent Union of South Africa. Durban is also
a holiday resort, especially in winter, as it has a

warm climate and beautiful beaches on the Indian Ocean. The ship was to stay there for six weeks during which time; I got to know it quite well. Unfortunately but like most places, it also had its darker side, which was apartheid, the forced discrimination against black people by the whites. If you were black, you were not allowed to go to a cinema, a bar, restaurants, beaches or anywhere where whites gathered, and to see a black woman with a baby in her arms standing outside a bus shelter in the pouring rain because she was not allowed inside, was something I had not been before and don't want to see again. About a fifth of the population of South Africa were white and of these more than half were Afrikaans of Dutch decent, the remaining having originally came from Britain.

Not everyone was against the coloureds or agreed with apartheid. I had met up with a girl, and we used to go to the playhouse cinema quite often, and one night we saw High Society with Louis Armstrong, and while this black singer was on, almost all of the audience stood up and applauded the screen. I found this very unusual and a massive contrast to what I had witnessed on the streets.

There was another time when this girl was having a bit of trouble with her servants. She lived in a house with a lot of land and the servants lived in a bungalow in the grounds. The man had torn up his wife's clothes and then thrown her out, so I was asked to go and sort it out. When I went along to see him, I discovered that he was an angry six foot six Zulu who had been drinking heavily. I knew I was in deep trouble and that the drunk could easily lay me out if he wished so in my eyes I only had two choices – bluff it out or run.

I've never been one to run away from a situation so I put on a brave face, and shouted at him to leave the premises and not come back until he had sobered up. To my surprise and relief, he meekly did and I have since reflected on how easy it was to assume the role of a white superior. Would he have walked away if he too had been white? Would my attitude have been different too? However, this was South Africa, which at the time was under white rule and a young Nelson Mandela was still six years away from being arrested for fighting against apartheid. The rest as they say is history.

One of the benefits of sailing back from Africa to London was a short stop at Las Palmas in the Canary Islands for bunkers. As this was a duty free port we could buy booze, baccy and gifts very cheap so it was a great opportunity to stock up.

Chapter 12

On the 19 November 1956, after another short spell at home, I set off again for London to join the SS Marsdale another veteran of action in World War 2.

The Marsdale a ship belonging to Houston and Company had been an armed merchant cruiser during the war. She had taken part in many convoys particularly on the UK to South Africa run. The captain had been on board her since she was built and he seemed to know every rivet in her well used hulk.

Our first port of call was on the west coast of Africa at Libito in Angola. Angola was officially a Portuguese Province, and they seemed to run it with an iron fist. The Africans who worked the ships all lived in an open warehouse in the dock area, and there were dozens of families crammed together with very little privacy. I thought this was the nearest thing to slavery that I had ever seen and I liked it even less than my experiences in South Africa. The Portuguese did not practice apartheid, there was no need to, but the Angolans were certainly not treated any better than in South Africa.

After a well deserved run ashore, we sailed south for Cape Town in Cape Province. The city is dominated by Table Mountain, which, I am very proud to say I climbed – all 3,563 feet of it – and from sea level! I believe they now have a cable car up there which saves a lot of effort.

After sailing around the Cape of Good Hope we arrived at Port Elizabeth where, it was rumoured that there was some unrest amongst the blacks against apartheid, thankfully, I never saw any trouble but there was also talk about the whites coming down from Rhodesia and further north in Kenya where they were fighting for independence. It was a very turbulent politically unsecure place to be as South Africa was to the final stand for white supremacy.

We sailed on from there into the Indian Ocean, bound for Beira in Mozambique. Mozambique was like Angola, a Province of Portugal and was to be the last large African country dominated by a European nation. Here however, there were no restrictions between the races and everyone seemed to live in harmony, so I enjoyed my time there before sailing this time for Germany.

Chapter 13

Due to the closure of the Suez Canal, we had to go the long way round, up the west coast of Africa, through Biscay and into the English Channel. After what seemed like a very long time at sea, we arrived in Hamburg.

Hamburg had been really hit hard during the war, but by now it had been built up to be quite a lively place. There was the famous Riberband, with all the clubs and German beer gardens and later on this is where the Beatles found fame. The whole crew really enjoyed our run ashore in Hamburg and we were all disappointed to pay off as the ship went into dry dock for repairs.

We then had to travel across Germany to the Hook of Holland to catch a ferry back to Harwich. Boarding the train in Hamburg, we found that there was standing room only in second class. Mischievously, we decided to go along to first class and make ourselves comfortable, after all, hadn't we just beaten the Germans in the war? When the conductor came, we refused to leave and after a while, when the train stopped at the station, the police came on board and threw us off the train. At that time, the British army was in every railway station, so we were taken to them and after phoning the British Consul we were told that 'we were not playing the game old chap', and were fined a few marks before being set free.

Our attempt at travelling without a valid ticket meant that we had to make our own way across the continent to the Hook of Holland. Our luggage had been left on the train with my trusted tool box, but we managed to bluff our way on a number of trains before reaching the ferry and crossing the North Sea to Harwich. Here, we found our luggage in a warehouse on the dockside then caught a train to London, found the Flying Angel Mission who put us up for the night. The next morning we went along to the Company Office, where we received the pay that was due to us, and returned home. By then I had signed a contract with the Shipping Federation, which meant that they would find me work on the ships, and in between ships, they would pay me a small retainer. So I spent four weeks at home before joining the Exmoor on the 24 April 1957.

I joined the ship in Newcastle, so once again we had a local crew and we were bound for Australia, via the Panama Canal. The Panama Canal was covered by the United States and they controlled a ten mile wide canal zone and in the 1950s and 60s there were riots against the continued American domination of the Canal Zone.

After a stormy Atlantic crossing, we arrived in Portobello, which was the entrance to the canal. This was a very cosmopolitan city with people of mixed European and American Indian descent, which they called Mestizos. After waiting for our turn, we moved on to the first set of three locks, which would take the ship up to the lakes level. The lake was reached by a nine mile long cutting through solid rocks. This was truly a great feat of civil engineering.

We sailed on across the Isthmus of Panama about fifty miles in all to reach the Pacific Ocean and then on to the long haul across the peaceful Pacific. This seemed to take forever and a day, with day after day of bright sunshine and smooth seas. So it was quite a while before we reached the Coral Sea and across the Great Barrier Reef to arrive in Cairns in Northern Queensland. Cairns at the time, was a bit of a one horse town, with wooden boardwalks for pavements and very little else, but it had a race course. I believe it is quite different now with it being close to the Great Barrier Reef, making it a centre for diving and all kinds of water sports.

We were there to load sugar, which kept us in Australia for the next six weeks.
The Dockers were mainly ex pats, and in Australia,

they had this thing called walkabout. They were a distinct breed of people who adopted a backpacker's style of life even though they did not seem to have any bags. Their total possessions seemed to amount to a pair of shorts, shoes and a shirt, and all they seemed to do was work the ships, go to the pub and sleep on the beach - in that order. The only thing they had an abundance of was excuses for not having to work. These ranged from the gangway was not safe, the wind was blowing sugar in their faces or they had to have a radio loudspeaker set up so they could hear the cricket commentary. Whatever they asked for, the ship had to comply with to keep the ship working, but apart from that, they did not seem to have a care in the world. I suppose that is one way of living.

We sailed on again across the Pacific Ocean for the Panama Canal, and saw very little, apart from the wonderful albatross, the mariner's bird. It seemed to follow us everywhere with its wing span of eleven foot, never landing and sleeping on the wing. We felt we were in good company with the glorious bird that never comes north of the Equator.

At length did cross an Albatross,
Thorough the fog it came;
As if it had been a Christian soul,
we hailed it in God's name.
It ate the food it ne'er had eat,
And round and round it flew.
The ice did split with a thunder-fit;
the helmsman steered us through!

The Rime of the Ancient Mariner (extract)

Chapter 14

We passed through the Panama Canal once more, passed Key West and up to the Eastern Seaboard of America to Canada. We docked in St John's, New Brunswick in the Bay of Fundy. St John's was too cold for my liking, so I was pleased when we left there bound for the sunny climes of the Gulf of Mexico. On the way there, we had to put up shifting boards that were needed to carry grain safely without it moving around the hold. We eventually arrived in the port of Tampico.

We spent Christmas and New Year there, where we all had a great time; the Mexicans sure know how to party. After we loaded up, we set sail for Antwerp in Belgium, and once more we set sail across the pond. About half way over, we ran into some real bad weather and during the night, I was called out to fix the steering gear hatch, which had been stove in with the potentially disastrous result of the steering gear compartment filling up with water. The Second Officer and Lookout came to help me as conditions on board the ship were terrible. We were running before a following sea, which is always dangerous. While we were fixing the hatch, she pooped one, which meant that the after end of the ship went under the water. The next thing I knew. I was completely thrown over the side. I remember thinking to myself that there was no way I could survive in this sea and that although life had not been so bad after all, I didn't want to die alone, in the dark and in the freezing cold water thousands of miles from my loved ones.

A second massive wave picked me up and threw me back onboard the ship. By then all hands had been called out, and someone grabbed me and put me into a paint locker. They also put the other injured seamen in. They were crying out in pain, they could not or would not answer me, the locker was half full of water and it was a very strange situation to be in. After a while the crew managed to get a life line rigged up to take us along to mid-ships. I point blank refused to go on a stretcher, as there was no way that I was going to be washed over the side again, so they hooked me up to a line and I walked along dazed but under my own steam. We all had been knocked about a fair bit, the Second Officer could not walk and the AB had a broken collarbone, which protruded through his blood stained shirt. My head was split open and my ribs were badly bruised, making it difficult to breath. My head looked pretty bad; you could see my skull through the two inch wide gash.

The Chief Steward, who also doubles as the ships doctor on most ships, tried to fix it, but he was a bit unsteady when he poured the antiseptic from the bottle into the wound, and most of it went into my eyes and not my gaping, blood stained head. Someone else on board a ship that is good with knives is the cook and so it was decided that he would do the job. He stitched my head up a few stitches in at a time, using a curved needle and pulling one stitch at a time until the gap was closed. He made a real good job of it and years after, he was always showing off his good work. We were made as comfortable as possible, but the weather was still bad and the next day the cadet was washed along the deck and broke his leg, so that meant that there were four of us laid up.

The storm got no better, so the Captain decided that as he could not put into the nearest port, which was the Azores, we would head up to the final port of discharge, which was Antwerp. On arrival, the four of us were taken to hospital for a check up and it was discovered that the Second Officer had a broken back. I felt really sorry for him because on the journey there we had been trying to make him walk to the toilet; he must have been in so much pain. The ABs collar bone was set by now and it was left to him whether to have it reset, but I don't think he bothered. The cadet's leg was put in plaster and my head was healing very nicely. I was x-rayed for my ribs and they were alright, although it was still very painful breathing, so after all that, we settled down to have a few days ashore in Antwerp albeit a rather subdued affair.

Chapter 15

After discharging the cargo, we sailed across the North Sea to dry dock on the River Tyne. After a full ten months at sea, I was due a spell ashore on leave. I enquired about compensation, but was told the same as I had been with the broken arms incident in Norway that it was an 'Act of God', now I was beginning to think that God did not like me at all. A later lucky escape made me change my mind however. I spent six weeks on leave this time before joining the Barror Gedes on the 25 April 1958.

I signed on again in my home port of South Shields and sailed once more across the pond for Galveston in the Gulf of Mexico. Galveston is a seaside town with shows along the pier and probably lots of people used it as a holiday resort. There were a lot of Mexicans there as it was close to the Border of Mexico. Anyway, it was a good run ashore for us, we were there to load sulphur and I believe this is mined underground, by being melted by steam and then pumped while molten to the surface. When loading it onto the ship, it was forever catching fire, so we had to be very careful and always on the alert for fires breaking out.

We sailed for Belfast in Northern Ireland, and

while I was there, I had a few drinks in the bars near the ship. I then decided to look for a night club, so I caught a taxi and asked the driver if he knew where the night life was. He drove me outside of town and dropped me at a derelict corner where there was a gang of men standing. Now lucky for me, a man and wife were passing and explained that they had seen this happened before, and these men were going to give me a right beating for no other reason except I was British. However, they lived near by so they took me home and got me a taxi back to the ship. I think I might not have survived that night at all, so there was another of my lives gone!

The next day, we paid off, and while waiting for the ferry to the UK, I called in for a drink in a dockside bar. I gave the barmaid a pound for a pint, which was quite a lot at that time; she never came back with the change. By then she was sitting with a crowd of locals and when I asked her for my change, one of them stood up and said, "I will give you a bit of advice, just forget about the change". I looked around and decided that discretion was the better part of valour and took his advice. By then, I was getting a bit fed up of this Irish hospitality, but in any event, I was never to return to Northern Ireland.

My next ship was to be the SS Troutpool and I signed on in South Shields on 9 July 1958. Before signing on, the Chief Officer explained that on the outward bound voyage, we were to put shifting boards up, and as the ship had never had them before, would I be willing to take the job on, so I said I would, providing he could get me an electric saw, a rarity at sea at the time.

Shifting boards had to be placed along the full length of the ship to prevent the grain moving over to one side when the ship rolled. This was necessary because when you loaded gain in bulk, it acted like water and the ship could have easily toppled over in a rough sea. We sailed to America and worked night and day to complete the job. When we arrived in Norfolk, Virginia the inspectors came on board, and the job was passed with flying colours, which was a great relief. We then set sail, this time for Leith in the Firth of Forth near Edinburgh where, when we docked, the Captain sent for me to tell me that he was very sorry, but they were sending a companies man to replace me. He said he was grateful for the work I had done, but it was out of his hands, I was without a ship again.

Chapter 16

My next ship was a little different, as it was in dry dock in Bremen Germany, I signed on in South Shields, myself and the rest of the crew had to fly out from Newcastle Airport to join the Dartmoor on 3 September 1958.

Newcastle Airport or as it was called then, Woolsington Airport ,was very small and there was no departure lounge as such, it was simply a Nissan hut with a set of scales. When they weighed us, they found that we were too heavy for the Dakota to take off and they had to send two of the catering staff by cross channel ferry. Flying in those days was quite daunting and a lot of the air safety considerations weren't even thought about. However, as we were soon to find out, life on board a ship was even more dangerous.

Arriving on board ship, we had to turn to straight away to lift the uprights out which had been used for shifting boards while the derricks were still up. On this ship, the deck beams could roll along to one end of the hold and when they were in position, they were held by a sliding bolt. Unfortunately and tragically, the bolt had been left out and so when making the lift with the lead lying over the beam, it had rolled along allowing the hatch to fall into the hold. The Deckhand guiding the lift was standing on the hatch and he fell into the hold, smashing his head in between decks with a horrendous thud on the way down. By the time we reached him, it was obvious that he was dead. The Chief Officer came down and ordered us to leave him to the shore people and to get on with our job. As the ship was sailing at midnight, not even a death on board stopped the work. Today, the Health and Safety Executive would have closed down the whole operation but I think they did things a little differently in those days.

We set sail for Recife, in Northern Brazil which is about eight degrees south of the Equator, and is with the rest of Brazil, a very happy place. The Brazilians seemed to live for music and football. Here we loaded magnize ore, which was very heavy and had to be loaded with a pitch fork into tubs and when the ship was loaded, the holds were only half full. We were bound for Rotterdam in the Netherlands.

We spent sometime there and found the place very pro British as they had been occupied by the Germans during the World War Two. Many of the locals told me stories about the occupation which clearly invoked very bitter memories.

Leaving Europe once more, we then sailed on to the Gulf of Mexico and up the Mississippi to New Orleans. The city is the largest in the state of Louisiana and lies about one hundred miles up the mighty river. Once governed by France, with a lot of people still speaking French, the city has recently been devasted by natural disasters. I remember it had some beautiful houses, with ornamental ironwork as well as being famous for its jazz scene. Although it was quite a good run ashore, it did have a dark side.

I happened to be coming back to the ship after a few drinks, and as I wanted a coffee, I asked the taxi driver to stop at a road side cafe. I asked him to come in with me, but as he was black, he said he would not be allowed, but I insisted, and we went in. The owner shouted 'get that black so and so out of here'. I found that very embarrassing, I had expected something like this in South Africa, but this was America, the land of the free, and I was beginning to think that this 'American Dream' that they like to call it was more like a nightmare.

After a few days we moved on up the river to the then capital Battenrouge. While there I used to call in to the nearest bar to the ship on the way into town. One night when I went in, the place was empty and I commented on this to one the barmen, he explained that there had been a bit of trouble that afternoon and the other barman had shot a Norwegian seaman. When I asked why he had not been arrested, he said quite casually that it was self defence. When I asked if the Norwegian has been armed, he said no, but he was not expected to know that! I thought then that this is what you see in cowboy films, but not in real life; however I never called in to that bar again. That was the second example of the dark side of New Orleans that I really didn't like.

After the ship was loaded, we then sailed down river and into the Gulf bound for the UK. While passing Key West, I set up a boom with a meat hook from the fridge with some rags wrapped around, on the end of the line. I fastened it to a biscuit tin laid along the deck so if a fish did bite, the tin would rattle loudly and alert us. Eventually there was a tremendous clatter and I rushed to haul in my catch. When I hauled it in, I had caught a beautiful Marlin. I gave it straight to the cook, but it tasted terrible and we could not eat it at all, so my fishing exploits ended there and then. We sailed across the Atlantic up the Irish Sea and into Liverpool where we paid off.

At Montevideo with a shipmate

Chapter 17

After a few weeks leave, I then joined the Temple Hall on the 20 March 1959 in South Shields, and so I had a mainly local crew once again. We then sailed on for the west coast of Africa. As was normal on this run, we had to pick up KRU boys, as they were known in Freetown, Sierra Leone. These lads were basically native Dockers employed to work the cargo in various ports we were to call in down the coast before arriving in Freetown. One of the most unusual tasks I had was to build a toilet for these men. This consisted of planks of wood laid out off the after end of the ship and fastened to the bollards. The men then did their business over the side. We used to fly the red ensign flag aft right next to the toilet – a bit disrespectful perhaps and the toilet facilities were quite precarious, but when you've got to go, you've got to go. We called the toilet the "African Ensign."

When we arrived in Freeport, the KRU boys came on board and what a colourful lot they were. There were about fifty of them and they would live in a tent on the hatch. They brought with them a huge cooking pot and I don't know what they put in it, but for the weeks they were on the ship, I would ask what's for dinner and they would always give me the same answer which was pepper soup.

We then sailed south for Takoraqi and Ghana and the Gulf of Guinea. Ghana had gained independence from Britain in 1957 and later it became a republic. In 1960 there were still a lot of British people working there in and around the harbour at Takoraqi. It was a happy place, and everyone seemed to mix well together. Later on of course there would be trouble when president Kwame Nkrumah would be overthrown and put into exile, but right then they were still on a high after gaining independence. I always remember the vivid colours of the men and women's clothing which reflected well the happy feelings I got from the town.

After loading the cargo, we moved on south to Lagos in Nigeria. Lagos itself was quite a large city with a big harbour, huge skyscrapers and a modern yacht club. From the modern huge city we moved towards a tiny village up the creek in the middle of the jungle called Sapele. After picking up the local pilot, we sailed quite a way up the creek with its views of wildlife and small clusters of primitive looking mud huts. It really made me appreciate my cramped home in South Shields which seemed a million miles away both physically and metaphorically and I wondered just how people managed to live in conditions like that.

Sapele was home to a large plywood factory and saw mills. There was also a lot of Brits working and living there. They had a nice club with a swimming pool and a pretty good standard of living. I enjoyed my stay there and had a real good time. You could also buy some bathtub gin, which was brewed in the jungle. Now this was really harsh stuff. One of the AB's was drinking it and it was so rough that it burnt his throat. He took all of the tomato sauce from the mess room to soften the effect to no avail. After he had been drinking for a couple of days, the Captain went aft and caught him, so he was logged, fined and told him to turn to the next day. The next day when he started work the boson put him over the side to paint the ship, however, after some pretty heavy drinking, he was in a very bad way. He was affected by the shakes and the DTs and couldn't hold on to the ladder properly. Unfortunately, he left go of the ladder and fell into the logs which we were loading. His head split open and he was dead when we got to him. I then made a cross and put on it
'John Robert Goodlad, South Shields, Age 56'.
We buried him up there in the jungle and carried on loading the logs. Life had to go on even after losing poor Robert.

The KRU boys were very good at manoeuvring the huge trees into the far corner of the holds. We also loaded a lot on the deck. I had to make a cat walk cross over them for the journey home. On the way we called in at Freetown to drop the KRU boys off and cut away the "African Ensign" before sailing for the continent. We then arrived in Rotterdam to discharge and while we were there, the company sent out a replacement AB for the man who was killed. After discharging we moved on north to Hamburg and Bramahaven in Germany to load cargo for China.

After spending time in Germany, which was beginning to liven up after the war years, we set off along the English Channel and through the Med for Alexandria in western Egypt, where we were to pick up some more cargo for China. On the way there, the replacement seamen started to complain that he could not sleep, because he was sleeping in the dead man's room and his ghost was banging the lockers and creating a right racket. I never heard it as my cabin was mid-ships, but the crew who lived there, all said they could and it was starting to spook them. The Chief Officer stepped in and suggested that he came back mid-ships to stay in the hospital; he also took him of watch keeping and put him on day work. He either was very frightened or he was an expert at getting out of hard work!

An uneventful passage saw us docking at Alexandria, which was famous for its lighthouse. This was a busy city with a tough reputation. The week before two American seamen had been killed and we were warned not to go ashore, but some of us went anyway, taking a horse drawn carriage to a club. A local gypsy came with us and told us that he was our guide; we said we didn't need a guide, but when he pulled out a huge knife and threatened us, we decided that a guide might be a good idea after all.

Chapter 18

After this, we sailed for the Suez Canal, through the red sea and into the Indian Ocean to head for Singapore to pick up bunkers, after which we moved on into the South China Sea and through the Formosa Straits. When passing through the straits you had to have a Union Jack painted on the deck to prove you were a British ship. At the time, the ex-leader of the Chinese Republic Chiag Kai-Shek had been over thrown and taken refuge in Formosa, later to become Taiwan. China was a communist country run by Mao Tse-Tung and the Americans were fighting anywhere where there was communism. The USA would not recognise China as a country and they said the real China was the Island of Formosa, and it was to be 1972 before China was allowed to become a member of the United Nations.

China at that time was in the middle of the Cultural Revolution and everyone was dressed the same in blue denim and it was hard to tell the difference between the sexes, and they were anti American. They were very pro British, and would invite us along to cocktail parties and to watch a show with everything provided for free, we just had to listen to what propaganda they told us about their country. They were very proud of their country, and proud people themselves. You could not give them anything at all, if you tried to tip them for serving you a drink, they would go out and buy you some sweets with the tip. One night I insisted that the old Rickshaw man, that had brought me back to the ship had a tip, and I would not accept the tip back. He took me to the police. They then solved the problem by making the Rickshaw man run around to use the tip up and explained that the people of China would not accept anything from anyone. One other thing they that they insisted on was an apology for anything at all and as long as they were to get the signed apology, everyone was happy. The Chief Officer kept a draw full ready. It was quite a different experience to see this country.

Sailing down the River Yangtze, we were hailed by a navy ship. One of our crew had been seen taking photos of the harbour which could have been classed as spying. They boarded us, found the camera and removed the film to which we opened the draw and presented them with a written apology before we were allowed to sail on to Tsingtad in the Yellow Sea, sometimes called China's sorrow.

Sailing back to England, I had Angus working for me, the man who had been disturbed by the ghost. One day I had to go on top of the boiler to free a blocked pipe. As it was very hot, I fastened a rope around my waist and asked Angus to pull me out if it got too much for me. When I did shout he was not there, with effort, I managed to get myself out and saw that he was pacing the deck. I noticed that he had a vacant look with piercing starry eyes. Without warning he lashed out at me and accused me of being a detective who was sent aboard to watch him. When I told the Chief Officer what had happened, he ordered me to remove all the fire axes in case Angus turned violent. When we reached Singapore, he was taken to see a doctor, who said he had a mental problem and we should try and get him home. Everything seemed to be going along alright and we passed through the Suez and Mediterranean. Angus would often come to my room to have a chat. He would tell me about where he lived in Stornaway in the Hebrides with this sister in a croft. He also liked to talk about his time on the whale catchers in the Atlantic. When I asked him about his problem, he would say that he was very near to an answer, but he just could not get there.

One morning, while I was on top of the mast house sounding the ship, the second steward, ran past shouting that he Angus was hanging and sure enough when I got aft Angus, had hung himself from a deck beam. When we cut him down, I had to start artificial respiration, which I had to do for four hours and with a seaman to relive me, we set about to try to save Angus's life. A Junior Officer came aft and said that he had been reading about the kiss of life method, by now his tongue was black and hanging right out and I told this officer that if he wanted to give him the kiss of life he was quite welcome to try it, but I certainly was not going to. Well after about three hours he was stone cold and the Captain said it was time we stopped. We then put into Lisbon in Portugal and handed him over to the care of the authorities, who heartlessly said we should have buried him at sea and saved them a lot of paperwork. Perhaps the ghost had taken over poor Angus's spirit.

The Temple Hall was sold to a Greek company in 1969 and she ran aground off the Canary Islands at Arrecife off the Lanzarote coast, I think she broke her back and now she is a popular wreck for divers. I wonder if they ever knew that there had been a ghost on board.

After this sad but eventful trip, we finally reached Liverpool and paid off. After spending Christmas at home, I next signed on to the Baltic Importer on New Years Day 1960. This was a very small ship and did not carry a dedicated Chippy, but rather a handyman and I was employed to repair all the windows and ports to save them the expense of the work being carried out by a ship repair firm. This was alright by me as I did not have any other duties, but as they were shorthanded, I did give them a hand with the tying up when entering and leaving harbour.

Chapter 19

My next adventure took me to colder climes when I sailed from the Thames to Helsinki, Finland in the Baltic Sea. To reach the Baltic, we went through the Kiel Canal which is in Germany. This was a good short cut as it saved going right around Denmark to reach the Baltic Sea. At that time of year it was bitterly cold and before reaching the port, we were frozen solid in ice, and had to wait our turn for the Russian icebreaker to free us, it seemed strange to see the people walking around the ship in the middle of the sea, but they were used to it as it was just a normal occurrence for them. When the icebreaker came, we then moved to Helsinki, but it was still difficult to get into the Harbour as we had to push the ice from the dockside to get alongside.

Finland at that time was a dry country and you could only have a couple of drinks if you were having a meal. It was also very old fashioned, for instance if you wanted a dance, you had to formally ask the girl, then help her out of her seat, then after the dance you had to escort her back and pull out the chair for her to sit down. There's something to be said about good old fashioned courting techniques but this was very hard work indeed.

After a couple of weeks we managed to get through

the Baltic back to the Kiel and the North Sea heading towards Hull. As I had not finished all the work I had to sign on again. So I spent a few days in Hull before sailing once more for Finland, this time the weather was no better, so once again we were stuck on ice. As the ship had a regular crew, they were doing a roaring trade with cheap wine, bought at home to sell in Helsinki. I suppose this was smuggling, but everyone seemed to turn a blind eye to it but at least I finished my work. We then sailed for London wharf and I paid off.

My next ship was the Cairnforth, which I joined in South Shields on the 22 February 1960.

We made our way across the North Sea for Antwerp in Belgium to load cargo for the United States. We spent some time in Antwerp, which was a great place to be. The most famous place was Danny's Bar in Skipper Street, but the whole place was pretty lively. After another cross Atlantic passage, we arrived in New York City. This was a great place to visit with its huge skyscrapers and the busy hustle and bustle of the city that never sleeps. The noise of police sirens and taxi cabs honking their horns meant that it was difficult to sleep even if you wanted to. While there I visited all the tourist spots like the Empire State Building, the Statue of Liberty and Central Park.

After sailing through the Panama Canal, we arrived at Long Beach in California. While I was there I missed the boat coming back to the ship and had to sleep in a doss house. This was a long dormitory with no privacy at all, so that was quite an experience. From there we sailed on north to Vancouver in British Columbia. I'm always amazed at some of the strange customs and laws I've encountered on my travels and they had some strange laws here too. For example, you were not allowed to go to the cinema on a Sunday and you could not go into the lounge of a bar without a woman. I tried to explain that the main reason to go into the lounge was to see the girls, but they still wouldn't let me in unaccompanied.

Another six week stay at Vancouver Island ensued to load timber due to the fact that the Dockers loaded one piece at a time and each parcel had to be marked with dye. There was not much to do there, but the scenery was very nice, so at least there was some consolation. We eventually loaded up with a full cargo hold as well as a high deck cargo and sailed on down the coast for Panama and onto the UK.

We arrived back in England destined for Manchester but to get there we had to go up the Manchester Ship Canal and go under the Bridges. We had to drop the top mast and take off the funnel at Runcorn and by looking at all the different funnels on the bank side; you could tell which ships were up there.

My next ship was to take me to the Far East and so I rejoined the Temple Hall on the 2 February 1960 in South Shields. We began our long journey to Japan and the city of Osaka on the mainland of Honshu. Osaka was Japan's second largest city. There was lots of night life here and you could enjoy some wonderful entertainment, all for the price of a drink. The Japanese people were very pro British at the time and they went out of their way to please us, they seemed to be such a gentle people that it was hard to imagine how ruthless they had been during the war. They were obsessed with cleanliness and no one was allowed in a house with shoes on. They also insisted on bathing every day. It was almost a religion for them.

Part of the Japanese culture reflected the fact that the male was very dominant and from birth the female was brought up primarily to please the man. I happened to take a Japanese girl to the cinema and during the show I asked her to go for some drinks, at the time I thought she had been away a long time. However I never said anything and carried on watching the film, when it ended the lights went up, I could see her face was covered in blood. I was really shocked and when I asked her what had happened, she said she had fallen down the stairs and she did not want to tell me in case it spoilt my show. I thought this was really crazy and could not imagine it happening anywhere else in the world. She was in a bad way, so I took her to hospital and they kept her in and I never saw her again. After enjoying a few weeks there we sailed back to the Thames and paid off.

Chapter 20

I joined the MV Orelia on the 8 February 1961 in Manchester. This was an iron ore ship owned by Holder Brothers. We sailed for Narvic in Sweden, the land of the blonde and the midnight sun. We only spent a couple of days there as it was always a quick turn around with that type of ship. We then sailed for Port Talbot in Wales. This was a huge steel works and at that time there were a lot of ships running there. As we sailed from there we discovered that we had an extra fireman on board. Evidently he could not read or write and had joined the ship by the funnel mark and as there were three ships of this company, he had joined the wrong ship. Luckily he was put ashore by the pilot cutter before we left the harbour. We went next to Conakry in Guinea and later on to Malica, a Spanish island off the coast of Morocco. I left the ship in Port Talbot and spent sometime at home before I joined the Elmina Palm in South Shields on the 17 July 1961, and sailed for the West Coast of Africa, calling in at Dakar in Senegal.

A lot of people spoke French having just gained independence three years previously. We moved on down the coast to Free Town to pick up the KRU boys again and after building the infamous African Ensign again, we sailed onto Lagos in Nigeria, which by this time had gained independence and it was funny to see the same men who had been asking for a (dash) handout were now declaring that they were customs men and other officials. After Lagos, we sailed on up the creeks to Sapali, again to spend some time in the club house, where everything seemed to be working the same as before, without the fighting that had happened in some other colonies. The trouble started much later in 1966.

When the army took over and a year later when Southern Nigeria rebelled and established their own state of Biafra, this caused a civil war and a famine through which many thousands died before the red cross and other charitable organisations could air lift food and other supplies to the region. Everyone was enjoying their new found freedom, and we helped them celebrate their independence in the best way we knew how to.

My next ship was a refrigerated ship also belonging to Holder Brothers, the Hardwick Grange. I joined her on the 24 November 1961. This I suppose was the happiest ship I was ever to sail on. She did a regular run to South America and the River Plate to pick up meat for Smithson's Market in London. On the way down via the South Atlantic the ship would be scrubbed spotlessly clean by the crew and they had to be very particular as it had to pass inspection before the meat was allowed on board. We also would pick up a load of fruit on the way home. We also carried fare paying passengers.

The Hardwick Grange

On one particular trip we had a number of race-horses on the foredeck. I enjoyed having them, I would give them water every morning while I was sounding the ship and they were always glad to see me. Our first port of call on the River Plate was Montevideo in Uruguay. This was just a small country, but a really good run ashore and I never found any trouble there at all, it was to be much later in 1970 before the military took over. After a few days we moved on up the River Plate to Buenos Aries to complete the loading. This was the largest city in the Southern Hemisphere and I was surprised at the number of lot of expats who lived there. The city even had an English newspaper. There was also a German Community and a lot of Nazi's were rumoured to have fled there after the war.

After getting to know the bars and oyster restaurants of Buenos Aries, we moved up the coast to Victoria in Brazil to load some pineapples for Marseilles. The run ashore not the best I have experienced, but in my opinion the French have never really accepted the English. While we were there, we had a watchman on the gangway. One night he stopped the second Steward from going ashore saying that he was too unsteady and that he was drunk. Not to be outdone, he then went forward to try and climb down the head rope. Unfortunately he never made it; he fell and broke his neck. The next day I had to go into his room to sort out his belongings and in doing so I found hypodermic needles and a quantity of drugs and although he had always seemed to be in a happy mood, no one ever thought he was a drug addict. There was not much of it about in those days. I've seen more of my fair share of death onboard ships but it was a dangerous occupation.

After Marseilles, we sailed on for the Royal Docks

in London to discharge the meat. This ship was to spend three weeks in port. After a spell at home on Tyneside, I rejoined the ship again and we sailed again for the River Plate to do more or less the same thing again. While we were in Buenos Aries, the Argentine navy went into the harbour and fired shells onto the palace to overthrow the president. What ever the trouble was, the streets were very lively with petrol bombs being thrown. I even managed to get myself arrested and thrown in jail. This consisted of a square cell with about twenty men in it. There was a marble bench to sit on, but as it was pretty full, I had to sit on the floor. Next to me was a Russian seaman and he kept me awake all night worrying about what was going to happen when he got back onboard his ship. The Russian on board who dealt with all disciplinary behaviour was very strict and at one time I believe that the prisoners were made to clean the streets of horse manure, but as they no longer used horses, this was not necessary.

We were treated fairly and they let us out the next afternoon. When I got back I was in trouble for being 'adrift' absent, but as this was a common occurrence, they were not too harsh on me.

As I was intending to say with this ship, I went home on leave, but a couple of days later, I received a telegram to tell me that there was a

Dockers strike and to beat this ship was sailing for France. By the time I got down to London, the ship had already sailed and my gear had been put ashore. So I then had to find another ship. I was moving from one ship to another until the next Holder Brothers ship came along with a vacancy for a Chippy. This was to be the Royston Grange. I joined her on the 26 June 1962. This was the sister ship to the Hardwick Grange and more or less did the same run to the River Plate. I still enjoyed my stay in Montevideo and Buenos Aries, but for whatever reason, I decided to leave the ship as I always had a bad uneasy feeling about the ship. Shortly after that, there was a collision with a tanker in the River Plate with a loss of all hands. The 7,113 ton Royston Grange, carrying 61 crew, twelve passengers including six women and a 5-year old child), and an Argentinean pilot, was bound from Buenos Aires to London with a cargo of chilled and frozen beef and butter. As she traversed the Punta Indio Channel, in dense fog at 5.40 a.m. she collided with the Liberian-registered tanker Tien Chee, carrying 20,000 tons of crude oil. The Tien Chee immediately burst into flames and a series of explosions rapidly carried the flames to the Royston Grange, which burned particularly hot due to the cargo of butter and the oil escaping from the Tien Chee. Most of the crew and passengers were asleep. Although the Royston Grange did not sink, every person on board was killed in the fire, most of them probably by carbon monoxide fumes emanating from the refrigeration tanks, which burst in the collision.

The ship was also an unusual design in that the bridge section, which contained the navigating officers and passengers accommodation, had no direct connection with the engine room, and was separated by a cargo hold from the aft engineer officers and crew accommodation above the main engine room. It would appear more probable that the crew and passengers were killed by the initial fierce fire caused by the crude oil leaking from the tanker and igniting after the collision, causing a very sudden high temperature with the fire consuming most of the oxygen. If the refrigerant containers and evaporation tanks had burst, it would have needed a very high temperature which would have probably been reached after the death of all persons on board. The Tien Chee also caught fire and ran aground, blocking all traffic in and out of the port of Buenos Aires. Eight of her crew, who were mostly Chinese, also died, but the remainder (and the Argentinean pilot) managed to abandon ship and were picked up by cutters of the Argentinean Navy.

The remains of the victims, mostly little more than ashes and charred bones (much of the flesh having been stripped from the bones by the hoses used by

Uruguayan tugs to put out the fire), were buried in six urns in two communal graves in the British cemetery in Montevideo on 20 May 1972 by the Rt. Reverend Jonas Ewing White, O.B.E, in the presence of 130 relatives who had been flown out to Uruguay by the ship's owners.

The report of the Liberian enquiry into the disaster concluded that the master and pilot of the Tien Chee, in an attempt to get enough water for her deep draught, had probably been navigating too far to the south of the channel and had pushed the Royston Grange onto the shelf that bordered it. The British ship had bounced off and into the tanker. The officers of the Royston Grange, it concluded, were probably not to blame, although there may have been some human error in attempting to avoid the collision. The master and pilot of the Tien Chee probably should not have entered the channel in the first place in the tidal conditions prevailing at the time. The report also criticised the lack of maintenance of the channel.

The Royston Grange was towed to Montevideo, and then to Spain, where her hulk was scrapped at Barcelona on 20 May 1979. The Tien Chee was also scrapped at Buenos Aires in August 1976.

The ill fated
"Royston Grange

Eric Gold

If this was to be called another act of God, then he had sure redeemed himself to me, and he had made sure that I was not on that ship at that time and thankfully, it was not my time yet.

Chapter 21

After spending four weeks at home, I was asked if I would like to join a ship in Genoa, Italy. I accepted as I thought it would be fun travelling through Europe, so I travelled first to Dover to catch the channel ferry then on to Paris to catch a train to Genoa.

I caught a taxi to Paris's main railway station. I offered the taxi driver double the fare if he got me there in time to catch the connecting train, but we got held up in traffic. Having missed the train, I decided to spend the night in Paris. At the time I was not worried about when or if I reached the ship as I was having a working holiday with my travel warrant. The train to Genoa was primitive as I was in a third class carriage which was very basic. My fellow passengers were very friendly feeding me sandwiches and wine and I thoroughly enjoyed their company on this long train ride to the Swiss border. I was in a bit of trouble as I did not have the correct papers for crossing the border, but after showing them my seaman discharge book, with my photograph in, they accepted this and I was free to move on. I arrived in Genoa on Friday afternoon and discovered that the British Consul had gone away and would not be back until Monday. This suited my plans as I had the whole weekend to myself in Genoa before joining the Kano Palm on the 3 September 1962.

The ship had a coloured crew with white officers and Petty Officers. This was becoming more and more common in the Merchant Navy. We sailed from there to the West Coast of Africa, once again to Ghana. First of all to Takoraqi to load palm oil for making soap, from there we moved on South to Accra, which was the Capital and what we called a surf port, as at the time there was no harbour so we had to anchor about a mile off and watch the cargo being transported in canoes with natives chanting to keep the rhythm which I found very impressive. I often wish the video camera had been invented then as this would have made a splendid movie.

Chapter 22

On arriving back in the UK, I was sent down to the Royal Docks in London to join a Royal Mail ship and as this was over the Christmas period, everyone had gone home to spend time with their families. I was left alone with only the shore watchman for company, so it was quite a lonely Christmas.

After the holidays, I signed on the Darro, on 27 December 1962. This was another refrigerated ship and a much older type with a wooden plug hatch, which had to be lifted out one at a time with the Derricks and they often got damaged in the process, and it meant a lot more work for me. We then sailed on down once again to the River Plate and Buenos Aries which was becoming like a home from home for me. I stayed with this ship for a couple of trips. The first trip was pretty uneventful and I spent my time going to football matches and horseracing. By the second trip, the political climate was changing again and they were having elections with Peron trying to come back after being in exile.

The streets were rather wild and as I did not want to miss any of the excitement, I went there among it, and some how ended up in jail again. The cell was even more crowded than the last time. There were two of the local homosexuals in the cell and whenever the guards came to the cell for whatever reason, they would drop their pants and try to rub up against them. It was a good laugh that night. When I got out the next day and got back to the ship, I was in big trouble again. I could not blame them, as the loading of the ship had been held up because of me. When we arrived back to the UK, I decided to leave as the ship was going to Tierra del Fuego, beside the Cape Horn and as this was a very cold and desolate place, I decided to try and find a ship to take me back to Japan.

After being back home for five weeks, I joined the Amberton on the 30 May 1963. This ship was bound for Japan, but first of all we had to load fertilizer in Argentina.

The time in Buenos passed pretty much the same as before. The only difference was that the ship was tied up a long way from the city, and I had to catch a train to meet my friend. While tied up there, unfortunately one of the crew fell off the gang plank while boarding, and was swept away by a strong current. His body was never found while we were there and I do not think they ever did recover it. This career was looking more and more dangerous to me. We eventually sailed from the River Plate for Japan. This was to prove to b a long journey as we were travelling east via the Cape of Good Hope off South Africa and for the next fifty two days we saw very little except for the ever faithful albatross. We had a short stay in Singapore for bunkers before finally arriving in Nagoya on the main Island of Honshu.

On arrival, the Captain after being pestered for subs by the crew decided to appoint the third officer to deal with it. This worked very well in Nagoya and the crew were able to draw their money daily, but I decided to draw all the money that was due to me, as I knew we were going to spend some time in port. We then moved on to Yokahama which is in Tokyo Bay. We all went ashore but the next day the third officer never turned up. This was a worry to most of us, but more so the Captain, but after a week he returned to the ship and declared that he had spent all the money and said he was sorry. His reasons for going AWOL were simple - he thought that this was a once in a lifetime chance to have a fling and he had done just that. The Captain decided not to report him to the authorities, but instead ordered him to stay on the ship and work to repay his debt, which he did as far as I know. He was still doing this when we all left the ship.

After a long stay in Yokahama, I left Japan for the last time to sail across the Pacific for the Panama Canal. We were in the locks on 22nd November

1963 and we heard that JF Kennedy had been shot in Houston. The Americans always used to say that everyone knew where they were when Kennedy was shot; and I do too.

We sailed across the Atlantic and arrived in Cardiff and I left the ship. I spent a further two months at home before joining the Lancashire on 20 February 1964 in Victoria Docks, London and sailed for Cape Town in South Africa. Apartheid was still being practiced and by then they had jailed Nelson Mandela. He was sent to Robin Island just off Cape Town and was to spend twenty seven years in jail. No one would have thought that on his release he would not only become the South African President, but would become one of the most respected figures in the whole world.

Like many I sailed on, this ship had a foreign crew, apart from the English Officers and I was the only PO on board. With the class system that was practiced in the navy, they left me pretty much on my own and as I had to get dressed up in uniform each evening for dinner, the whole thing did not appeal to me at all, so on arrival in the UK, I left the ship at Avonmouth to look for something different. After four weeks leave, I joined a tanker, The Hamilton on the 1 June 1964 in South Shields and as this was a crew from my home town, I knew best part of them so it was the complete opposite to the last ship and I had plenty of friends on board.

We sailed from the Tyne first of all for Casablanca in Morocco, at first glance this seemed to be a very dodgy place with long back alley ways teeming with men, but we never had much trouble and the night life was lively enough. From there we sailed across the pond for Maracaibo Lake in Venezuela. This was a beautiful lake surrounded with mountains and we were to run from there to the Island of Curacao, belonging to the Netherlands. For the next month both places were a good run ashore and everyone enjoyed it. After that we made various trips up and down the east coast of America, and once again back to Buenos Aries to stay for engine repairs, and another trip to Kennedy Airport with aviation spirit, before sailing back to the UK to pay off.

Because I had been away for a fairly long time, I decided to take a couple of months off. This was the time of the swinging sixties. The gambling laws had been relaxed and clubs were springing up all over the place, not just in my home town, but all over the country, and everyone appeared to be going out and enjoying themselves. One Prime Minister said later on, that we had never had it so good and I for one believed that they seemed to have found the answer on how to enjoy life. It was not to last and since those days we seem to have gone backwards.

However I had to work to do, so I travelled down to Avonmouth to join the RMS Caledonia on the 21 January 1965. This was a passenger ship belonging to Anchor Line of Glasgow. This was completely different to what I had been used to, it had an Indian Crew of three hundred, British Officers, Petty Officers and Quarter Masters who used to steer the ship. It also carried a plumber, which was big help to me as in the past; I had to do all the plumbing work on ships.

This was one of three ships that the Anchor Line had on regular runs to India, and it proved to be a very good job for me. From Avonmouth, we sailed up to Liverpool to pick up passengers. In those days, when a passenger ship sailed it was something of an occasion with a brass band and streamers from ship to shore, which made it all the more special. From Liverpool we sailed through the Med for the Suez Canal, where we picked up more passengers from Aden. Going through the Red Sea we received an SOS from a boat that was sinking. It turned out that this was a film crew doing some underwater filming for a documentary and it had hit a reef, so we launched a lifeboat and picked them up. After calling at Aden for bunkers, we sailed on for Bombay in India. After docking and clearing the ship, we had to lay up and wait for about three weeks, before picking up the next set of passengers for the UK.

Chapter 23

After spending another two weeks at home, I rejoined the ship in Glasgow to do more or less the same thing. After passing through the Suez Canal for bunkers as was the routine at the time as the South Yemen Gorillas were fighting the British for independence. It was a very tough campaign and the British Army had suffered a lot of casualties. While we were there, bombs were going off all over town and we were warned not to go to town. I went ashore to buy a watch for a girl back home. On going down the street a car blew up in front of me and two British army lads grabbed me and frog marched me into the nearest bar. They were acting a bit jumpy, but who could blame them. It did not take them long to clear me and I went back on my way, bought the watch and got back to the ship safely. On this particular trip, we had to call in at Karachi in Pakistan to drop off some passengers. At the time, Pakistan was at war with India and some of the passengers as well as the crew were Indian. This was a very strange situation indeed, but everything went alright, although no one was allowed to go ashore. We then sailed east to Bombay where I discovered that the Navy's biggest ships were put into dry dock in case they were sunk. This seemed to me to be a funny old war to say the least. I was to spend another three

weeks in Bombay before taking on more
passengers for Liverpool.

On the way home I was targeted by card sharks,
working the trains. Luckily I had heard about
this from a seaman who had lost all of his money,
which could amount to more than a year's wages.
They operated by placing a con man by the ticket
office and if you got a ticket by means of a railway
warrant, he would know you had just paid off a
ship. This is exactly what happened to me when
I boarded the train and sat in an empty carriage.
This man came and joined me, he told me he was a
farmer from Leeds and had been down to sell a few
sheep. He was quite good company, but that was
his job, to gain my confidence, but of course I did
not know that at that time further down the line,
another three of the gang got on the train and
joined us. One of them was very funny and
supposedly half drunk, and said he was going up
North to play in a competition for his local club.
This game was called shuffle board and was played
on a big board, but as there was not enough room
here, he would try to show us with just three cards.
Now as I had been fore warned, I knew exactly
what their game was. However they kept betting
between themselves and the man with the cards
seemed to be so clumsy; it appeared to be very easy
to beat him. The farmer, who had made friends

with me, kept trying to tell me how easy he would be to beat, but I refused to be drawn in and after a while, the dealer let a card fall beside me and asked me to pass it back. When I did, he then accused me of bending the corner to allow the others to win. Now by this time, I was really worried and did not know what to do. But what I did do was to look at each one individually and say come on lads give me a break and to my surprise, they all stood up and shook my hand and said have a good leave Geordie, and left the train in Manchester.

I then went to the train guard and told him what had happened, but he told me that he had a wife and family and he refused to report it as he had heard of the gang and was afraid of repercussions. I considered myself to be very lucky to get away with that. After a couple of weeks at home, I went back to join the Caledonia in Birkenhead before we embarked on our regular run up the Western Isles of Scotland. This made a very pleasant change, as it is very beautiful up there.

This trip was corporate entertainment for a lot of the Reps and everything was free, including the drink and to see them ordering whisky from the bar to pour into empty bottles was quite funny. It just showed what human nature was when you could get something for nothing. After a couple of days we went back to Liverpool to pick up passengers for India. It was more or less the same voyage, there was still fighting in Aden, and it was another year before it gained independence. While we were in India, we were informed that the company had been taken over by Runciman and he intended to scrap the whole fleet. We thought it was asset stripping, as there were a lot of premises belonging to them there, but the truth was that the end was in sight for passenger ships, as they had been more or less taken over by air travel, but it was still very sad for a lot of the crew, as some of them had been there for twenty years or more. Indeed, I think the Chief Officer had been waiting that length of time for his own command, and so it was with a lot of heavy hearts that we sailed from Bombay for the last time, and even though the trip was pretty un-eventful, I'll never forget it.

We eventually arrived back in the UK and finally left the ship in Glasgow, on the 26 November 1965. I had another two months holiday before joining the Beaver Fir on the 9 February 1966 in Liver-pool. This was one of the few ships owned by Canadian Pacific, which ran regular trips to Canada, mainly Montreal, so off we sailed across the North Atlantic.

I had been at sea sometime now and had seen quite a few storms, but I had never come across the mountainous seas that I was to experience on this trip. It was difficult to sit and eat and at night you had to try and wedge yourself in your bunk. The captain had brought his wife with him and she was really frightened as well as being violently seasick and she never left the chart room. When we reached Montreal, she left the ship and flew home and said she would never set foot on a ship again. I stayed on this ship for a further three trips and did a bit of relieving on the Empress ships belonging to the company. These were passenger ships that ran regular trips to Canada, but once again being forced out of business by air travel. On the last trip we called in at Quebec on the St Lawrence I found this a very strange run ashore as the people would only speak French. I don't think they ever forgave us for capturing the city in 1759. We moved from there up river for about 160 miles to Montreal. This place was great and I enjoyed the times that I spent there. On the last trip there was a Dockers strike so to beat the strike, we moved on through the sea way to Detroit City in Michigan. Going through the seaway, you could hear the thunder of the Niagara Falls, but I never got to see them. While in Detroit, we were asked if we would like to discharge the ship and to be paid by the American shore boss. Well of course we all agreed to this, I was put in charge of a gang and part of the cargo was pavilions for the expo, which was being held in Canada the following year.

Detroit is one of the most important car manufacturing centres in the world and the music industry calls it Motown. While I did not make music there, I did manage to make a few dollars and after the three trips on the Beaver Fur, I finally sailed for Liverpool to pay off for the last time.

Looking back over the years, I have thoroughly enjoyed my time at sea and I consider myself lucky to have seen all the different countries gain their independence and witness all the changes that have happened in the world. My discharge papers tell the stories of where I have been and my memories tell me what I've done.

One has to ask, have the changes made anyone any better off or indeed are we better off than we were in the sixties? I will leave you to be the judge, as for me, I was to settle down to work ashore and try something new. But always remember that whenever there is a gathering of people, there will always be someone willing to swing the lamp.

Alan Mulvain August 2011